PYTHON FOR BEGINNERS

COMPILED BY UMAR AFTAB

Introduction:

Python is one of the most popular programming languages used for data analytics. It is a high-level language that is easy to read, write, and understand. It has a large and active community that contributes to its libraries, making it a powerful tool for data analytics. Python provides several libraries such as NumPy, Pandas, Matplotlib, Scikit-learn, etc., that make it easy to perform various data analysis tasks. This e-book will provide an introduction to Python and its libraries.

Section 1: Getting started with Python

This chapter will introduce Python and its basic syntax. We will discuss how to install Python on your machine and how to use Python's Integrated Development Environment (IDE) to write and run code. We will also cover the fundamental concepts of Python, such as variables, data types, and control structures.

- Chapter 1: Getting started with Python
- Chapter 2: Data Types and Structures in Python
- Chapter 3: Control Flow and Functions in Python
- Chapter 4: Data Structures in Python
- Chapter 5: Control Flow in Python
- Chapter 6: Functions in Python
- Chapter 7: Object-Oriented Programming in Python
- Chapter 8: Error Handling and Debugging in Python
- Chapter 9: Working with Files in Python

Section 2: Introduction to NumPy

NumPy is a library for scientific computing in Python. It provides support for large, multi-dimensional arrays and matrices, and high-level mathematical functions to operate on these arrays. In this chapter, we will discuss the basics of NumPy, including how to create and manipulate arrays, perform basic mathematical operations, and how to use indexing and slicing to extract data from arrays.

Section 3: Introduction to Pandas

Pandas is a library for data manipulation and analysis in Python. It provides data structures for efficiently storing and manipulating large datasets, and functions for data cleaning, merging, and transformation. In this chapter, we will introduce Pandas, including how to create and manipulate data frames, handle missing data, and perform groupby operations.

Section 4: Introduction to Data Visualization with Matplotlib

Matplotlib is a library for creating static, animated, and interactive visualizations in Python. It provides support for creating a wide range of plots, including line, bar, scatter, and histogram plots. In this chapter, we will explore Matplotlib, including how to create basic plots, customize plot styles, and use subplots to create multiple plots in a single figure.

Section 5: Introduction to Machine Learning with Scikit-learn

Scikit-learn is a library for machine learning in Python. It provides a range of supervised and unsupervised learning algorithms, including regression, classification, clustering, and dimensionality reduction. In this chapter, we will introduce Scikit-learn, including how to preprocess data, split data into training and testing sets, and how to use Scikit-learn to train and evaluate machine learning models.

SECTION 1

Chapter 1: Getting started with Python

Python is a high-level, general-purpose programming language that is widely used in data analytics, web development, and scientific computing. It is an interpreted language, which means that the code is executed directly without the need for a compilation step. This makes it easy to write and test code quickly, making it an excellent choice for data analytics.

In this chapter, we will introduce Python and its basic syntax. We will discuss how to install Python on your machine and how to use Python's Integrated Development Environment (IDE) to write and run code. We will also cover the fundamental concepts of Python, such as variables, data types, and control structures.

Installing Python

Before you can start using Python, you need to install it on your machine. Python is available for download from the official website, python.org. There are two main versions of Python, Python 2 and Python 3. It is recommended to use Python 3 as Python 2 is no longer supported.

Once you have downloaded the appropriate version for your operating system, run the installer and follow the prompts to install Python on your machine. You can also install Python using a package manager such as pip or conda.

Python IDEs

Once you have installed Python, you can start writing and running code. Python comes with a built-in interpreter that can be used to execute Python code directly in the command prompt or terminal. However, most developers prefer to use an Integrated Development Environment (IDE) to write and run Python code.

Some popular Python IDEs include:

1. PyCharm—a powerful, full-featured IDE for Python development.
2. Spyder—a lightweight IDE that is easy to use and includes a range of scientific computing libraries.
3. Visual Studio Code—a popular code editor that has excellent support for Python development.

Variables and Data Types

In Python, variables are used to store values such as numbers, strings, and Boolean values. To assign a value to a variable, you can use the equals sign (=).

For example, to assign the value 10 to a variable called "x", you can write:

```
x = 10
```

Python has several built-in data types, including:

1. Integers—whole numbers, such as 1, 2, 3, etc.
2. Floats—decimal numbers, such as 1.0, 2.5, etc.
3. Strings—text data, enclosed in single or double quotes, such as "hello" or 'world'.
4. Booleans—true or false values, represented by the keywords True and False.

Control Structures

Control structures are used to control the flow of execution in a Python program. The two most common control structures are if statements and loops.

If statements are used to test conditions and execute different code based on the result. For example, to test if a variable x is greater than 10, you can write:

```
if x > 10:
    print("x is greater than 10")
else:
    print("x is less than or equal to 10")
```

Loops are used to repeat a block of code multiple times. The two most common types of loops in Python are for loops and while loops. For example, to print the numbers 1 to 10, you can use a for loop:

```
for i in range(1, 11):
    print(i)
```

Conclusion

In this chapter, we introduced Python and its basic syntax. We discussed how to install Python on your machine and how to use Python's Integrated Development Environment (IDE) to write and run code. We also covered the fundamental concepts of Python, such as variables, data types, and control structures.

Chapter 2: Data Types and Structures in Python

In this chapter, we will dive deeper into the different data types and structures available in Python. We will discuss how to use these data types and structures to perform data analysis tasks.

Data Types

As we discussed in the previous chapter, Python has several built-in data types, including integers, floats, strings, and Booleans. However, Python also has several other data types that are commonly used in data analysis.

1. Lists—a list is a collection of items, enclosed in square brackets, separated by commas. Lists can contain items of different data types.

```
my_list = [1, 2, 3, "four", 5.0]
```

2 .Tuples—a tuple is similar to a list, but once created, it cannot be modified. Tuples are enclosed in parentheses.

```
my_tuple = (1, 2, 3, "four", 5.0)
```

3. Dictionaries—a dictionary is a collection of key-value pairs, enclosed in curly braces. Dictionaries can contain items of different data types.

```
my_dict = {"name": "John", "age": 30, "gender": "male"}
```

4. Sets—a set is an unordered collection of unique items, enclosed in curly braces.

```
my_set = {1, 2, 3, 4, 5}
```

Data Structures

In addition to data types, Python also has several built-in data structures that are useful for data analysis.

1. Arrays—an array is a collection of items of the same data type. Arrays can be created using the numpy library.

```
import numpy as np
my_array = np.array([1, 2, 3, 4, 5])
```

2. DataFrames—a DataFrame is a two-dimensional table that can be used to store and manipulate data. DataFrames can be created using the pandas library.

```
import pandas as pd
data = {"name": ["John", "Mary", "Bob"], "age": [30, 25, 35]}
df = pd.DataFrame(data)
```

3. Series—a Series is a one-dimensional array-like object that can be used to store and manipulate data. Series can be created using the pandas library.

```
import pandas as pd
data = [1, 2, 3, 4, 5]
s = pd.Series(data)
```

Indexing and Slicing

To access specific elements of a data type or structure, we can use indexing and slicing. Indexing is used to access a specific element of a data type or structure, while slicing is used to access a range of elements.

For example, to access the first element of a list, we can use indexing:

```
my_list = [1, 2, 3, "four", 5.0]
print(my_list[0]) # Output: 1
```

To access a range of elements from a list, we can use slicing:

```
my_list = [1, 2, 3, "four", 5.0]
print(my_list[1:4]) # Output: [2, 3, "four"]
```

Conclusion

In this chapter, we discussed the different data types and structures available in Python, including lists, tuples, dictionaries, sets, arrays, DataFrames, and Series. We also discussed how to use indexing and slicing to access specific elements of a data type or structure. With this knowledge, we can start using Python to perform data analysis tasks.

Chapter 3: Control Flow and Functions in Python

In this chapter, we will explore the concept of control flow in Python and how we can use it to manipulate data. We will also learn about functions and how they can be used to modularize code.

Control Flow

Control flow refers to the order in which statements are executed in a program. In Python, we can use control flow statements to control the order of execution of our code.

1. Conditional Statements—We use conditional statements to execute code only when certain conditions are met. The two most common conditional statements in Python are the if and else statements.

```
x = 10
if x > 5:
    print("x is greater than 5")
else:
    print("x is less than or equal to 5")
```

2. Loops—We use loops to execute the same block of code multiple times. The two most common types of loops in Python are the for loop and the while loop.

```
for i in range(5):
    print(i)
    i = 0
    while i < 5:
        print(i)
        i += 1
```

Functions

Functions are reusable blocks of code that perform a specific task. Functions can be called multiple times with different input values, making them a powerful tool for modularizing code.

1. Defining Functions—We define functions using the def keyword, followed by the function name and the parameters in parentheses. The code block that defines the function is indented.

```
def add_numbers(x, y):
    result = x + y
    return result
```

2. Calling Functions—We call functions by using the function name, followed by the input values in parentheses.

```
result = add_numbers(5, 10)
print(result) # Output: 15
```

3. Default Parameters—We can define default parameters for functions, which are used if no value is provided for that parameter.

```
def greet(name="John"):
    print("Hello, " + name)
    greet() # Output: Hello, John
    greet("Mary") # Output: Hello, Mary
```

Conclusion

In this chapter, we discussed control flow statements in Python, including conditional statements and loops. We also learned about functions and how they can be used to modularize code. With this knowledge, we can start writing more complex programs that manipulate data in sophisticated ways.

Chapter 4 : Input and Output in Python

In this chapter, we will explore how to read input from users and how to write output to files in Python.

1. Input—We use the `input()` function to read input from the user. The input function takes a prompt as an argument and returns the user's input as a string.

```
name = input("What is your name?")
print("Hello, " + name)
```

2. Output—We use the `print()` function to write output to the console. We can use formatting codes such as `%d` for integers and `%f` for floats to format the output.

```
x = 5
y = 10
print("The sum of %d and %d is %d" % (x, y, x+y))
```

3. File Input and Output—We can also read input from files and write output to files in Python. We use the `open()` function to open a file, and we can specify whether we want to read from the file, write to the file, or both.

```
# Writing to a file
with open("my_file.txt", "w") as file:
    file.write("Hello, world!")
# Reading from a file
with open("my_file.txt", "r") as file:
    contents = file.read()
    print(contents)
```

4. CSV Files—CSV (Comma Separated Values) files are a common file format for storing tabular data. We can use the `csv` module to read and write CSV files in Python.

```
import csv
# Writing to a CSV file
with open("my_data.csv", "w", newline="") as file:
    writer = csv.writer(file)
    writer.writerow(["Name", "Age", "City"])
    writer.writerow(["John", 30, "New York"])
    writer.writerow(["Mary", 25, "Chicago"])
# Reading from a CSV file
with open("my_data.csv", "r") as file:
    reader = csv.reader(file)
    for row in reader:
        print(row)
```

Conclusion

In this chapter, we explored how to read input from users and write output to files in Python. We also learned how to work with CSV files using the `csv` module. With this knowledge, we can start building more complex programs that read and write data from various sources, including user input and files.

Chapter 5: Control Flow in Python

In this chapter, we will explore the different control flow statements in Python and how they can be used to control the flow of execution in a program.

1. Conditional Statements—We use conditional statements to execute code only if a certain condition is met. The if, elif, and else keywords are used to construct conditional statements.

```python
x = 5
if x > 0:
    print("x is positive")
elif x < 0:
    print("x is negative")
else:
    print("x is zero")
```

2. Loops—We use loops to execute a block of code repeatedly. There are two types of loops in Python: for loops and while loops.

```python
# For loop
fruits = ["apple", "banana", "cherry"]
for fruit in fruits:
    print(fruit)
# While loop
i = 0
while i < 5:
    print(i)
    i += 1
```

3. Break and Continue Statements—We use the break and continue statements to alter the flow of a loop. break is used to exit the loop entirely, while continue is used to skip the current iteration and move on to the next one.

```python
# Break statement
fruits = ["apple", "banana", "cherry"]
for fruit in fruits:
    if fruit == "banana":
        break
    print(fruit)

# Continue statement
for i in range(10):
    if i % 2 == 0:
        continue
    print(i)
```

4. Exception Handling—We use exception handling to handle errors that occur during the execution of a program. The try, except, else, and finally keywords are used to construct exception handling statements.

```
try:
    x = int(input("Enter a number: "))
    print("The reciprocal of", x, "is", 1/x)
except ValueError:
    print("Invalid input")
except ZeroDivisionError:
    print("Cannot divide by zero")
else:
    print("No exceptions raised")
finally:
    print("Done")
```

Conclusion

In this chapter, we explored the different control flow statements in Python, including conditional statements, loops, break and continue statements, and exception handling. These statements are essential for controlling the flow of execution in a program and handling errors that may occur during the execution. With this knowledge, we can start building more complex programs that make use of these control flow statements to execute code conditionally, iterate over data, and handle errors.

Chapter 6: Functions in Python

In this chapter, we will explore functions in Python, which allow us to break our code into reusable and modular pieces.

1. Defining a Function—We define a function using the `def` keyword, followed by the function name, a set of parentheses, and a colon. The code that makes up the function is then indented.

```
def greet(name):
    print("Hello, " + name)
```

2. Calling a Function—We call a function by using its name followed by a set of parentheses, and any arguments that the function expects.

```
greet("John")
```

3. Arguments—Functions can take one or more arguments, which are values that are passed into the function when it is called. Arguments can be either positional or keyword arguments.

```
# Positional Arguments
def add(x, y):
    return x + y
result = add(5, 10)
# Keyword Arguments
def multiply(x, y=1):
    return x * y
result = multiply(5, y=10)
```

4. Return Values—Functions can return a value using the `return` keyword. If a function does not return a value, it returns `None` by default.

```
def add(x, y):
    return x + y
    result = add(5, 10)
    print(result)
```

5. Scope—The scope of a variable refers to the part of the program where the variable is accessible. Variables defined inside a function have local scope and can only be accessed within that function.

```
def outer_function():
    x = 1
def inner_function():
        x = 2
        print("Inner function:", x)
    inner_function()
    print("Outer function:", x)
outer_function()
```

6. Lambda Functions—Lambda functions are a way to create small anonymous functions in Python. They are useful for creating small functions that are only needed once.

```python
multiply = lambda x, y: x * y
result = multiply(5, 10)
print(result)
```

Conclusion

In this chapter, we explored functions in Python, including how to define and call functions, pass arguments, and return values. We also looked at the scope of variables and how it affects the accessibility of variables in our program. Finally, we explored lambda functions, which allow us to create small anonymous functions. With this knowledge, we can start building more complex programs that make use of functions to break our code into modular and reusable pieces.

Chapter 7: Object-Oriented Programming in Python

In this chapter, we will explore Object-Oriented Programming (OOP) in Python, which is a way of programming that focuses on objects and their interactions.

1. Classes—Classes are the blueprints for creating objects in Python. They define the properties and methods that objects of that class will have.

```
class Person:
    def __init__(self, name, age):
        self.name = name
        self.age = age
    def greet(self):
        print(f"Hello, my name is {self.name} and I'm {self.age} years old.")
```

2. Objects—Objects are instances of a class. They have their own set of properties and methods defined by the class.

```
person1 = Person("John", 30)
person1.greet()
```

3. Inheritance—Inheritance is a way of creating a new class based on an existing class. The new class, known as the child class, inherits all the properties and methods of the parent class.

```
class Student(Person):
    def __init__(self, name, age, major):
        super().__init__(name, age)
        self.major = major
    def study(self):
        print(f"I'm studying {self.major}.")
student1 = Student("Jane", 20, "Computer Science")
student1.greet()
student1.study()
```

4. Polymorphism—Polymorphism is the ability of objects of different classes to be used interchangeably.

```
def introduce(person):
    person.greet()
    person2 = Student("Bob", 25, "Biology")
introduce(person2)
```

5. Encapsulation—Encapsulation is the idea of hiding the implementation details of a class from the outside world, and only exposing a public interface.

```
class BankAccount:
    def __init__(self, balance):
        self.__balance = balance
    def deposit(self, amount):
        self.__balance += amount
```

```
    def withdraw(self, amount):
        if amount > self.__balance:
            print("Insufficient funds.")
        else:
            self.__balance -= amount
    def get_balance(self):
        return self.__balance
account1 = BankAccount(1000)
account1.withdraw(500)
print(account1.get_balance())
```

Conclusion

In this chapter, we explored Object-Oriented Programming in Python, including how to define and use classes, create objects, use inheritance and polymorphism, and encapsulate our code. With OOP, we can write more modular and reusable code that is easier to maintain and extend. Understanding OOP is essential for building complex programs and applications in Python.

Chapter 8: Error Handling and Debugging in Python

In this chapter, we will explore how to handle errors and debug our Python code. Error handling and debugging are crucial skills for any programmer, as it helps identify and resolve issues in our code.

1. Exceptions—Exceptions are errors that occur during the execution of our Python program. We can handle these exceptions using the try and except statements.

```
try:
    x = 1 / 0
except ZeroDivisionError:
    print("Cannot divide by zero.")
```

2. Handling Multiple Exceptions—We can handle multiple exceptions in a single try block using multiple except statements.

```
try:
    x = int(input("Enter a number: "))
    y = 1 / x
except ValueError:
    print("Invalid input.")
except ZeroDivisionError:
    print("Cannot divide by zero.")
```

3. Raising Exceptions—We can raise our own exceptions using the raise statement.

```
def divide(x, y):
    if y == 0:
        raise ZeroDivisionError("Cannot divide by zero.")
    return x / y
```

4. Debugging—Debugging is the process of identifying and resolving errors in our code. We can use the print statement to debug our code by printing out the values of variables at certain points in our program.

```
def calculate_total_cost(price, quantity):
    tax_rate = 0.1
    total_cost = price * quantity
    print(f"Price: {price}")
    print(f"Quantity: {quantity}")
    print(f"Tax Rate: {tax_rate}")
    print(f"Total Cost: {total_cost}")
    return total_cost + (total_cost * tax_rate)
calculate_total_cost(10, "five")
```

5. Debugging Tools—Python provides several built-in tools for debugging, including the pdb module for interactive debugging, and the `logging` module for logging debug messages.

```
import logging
logging.basicConfig(level=logging.DEBUG)
  def divide(x, y):
    logging.debug(f"divide({x}, {y})")
    if y == 0:
        logging.error("Cannot divide by zero.")
        return None
    return x / y
```

Conclusion

In this chapter, we explored how to handle errors and debug our Python code using exception handling, raising exceptions, and various debugging techniques such as print statements, interactive debugging, and logging. By mastering these skills, we can write more robust and reliable code, and troubleshoot errors quickly and efficiently.

Chapter 9: Working with Files in Python

In this chapter, we will explore how to work with files in Python. Working with files is a common task in programming, and Python provides several built-in functions and modules that make it easy to read from and write to files.

1. Opening and Closing Files—Before we can read from or write to a file, we need to open it using the open() function. We can specify the file mode (read, write, append, etc.) using the second argument.

```
file = open("example.txt", "w")
file.write("Hello, world!")
file.close()
```

2. Reading from Files—We can read from a file using the read() method. This method returns the entire contents of the file as a string.

```
file = open("example.txt", "r")
contents = file.read()
print(contents)
file.close()
```

3. Reading Lines from Files—We can read lines from a file using the readline() method. This method returns a single line from the file as a string.

```
file = open("example.txt", "r")
line1 = file.readline()
line2 = file.readline()
print(line1)
print(line2)
file.close()
```

4. Writing to Files—We can write to a file using the write() method. This method writes a string to the file.

```
file = open("example.txt", "w")
file.write("Line 1\n")
file.write("Line 2\n")
file.close()
```

5. Appending to Files—We can append to a file using the append() method. This method adds a string to the end of the file.

```
file = open("example.txt", "a")
file.write("Line 3\n")
file.write("Line 4\n")
file.close()
```

6. Using `with` Statements - We can use `with` statements to automatically close files after we are done working with them. This is a safer and more convenient way to work with files.

```python
with open("example.txt", "r") as file:
    contents = file.read()
    print(contents)
```

7. Working with Binary Files—We can open and read from binary files using the `rb` mode, and write to binary files using the `wb` mode.

```python
with open("example.jpg", "rb") as file:
    contents = file.read()
    print(len(contents))
```

Conclusion

In this chapter, we explored how to work with files in Python using built-in functions and modules. We learned how to open and close files, read from and write to files, and work with binary files. By mastering these skills, we can read and write files of different types and formats, and perform common file operations efficiently and effectively.

SECTION 2

NumPy, short for Numerical Python, is a fundamental package in Python used for numerical computing. It provides powerful tools for manipulating large multi-dimensional arrays and matrices, along with a large library of mathematical functions for performing operations on these arrays. NumPy is widely used in scientific computing, data analysis, and machine learning applications.

Here are some of the key features and benefits of using NumPy:

1. Multi-dimensional array support: NumPy provides an efficient array object that can hold and manipulate large multi-dimensional arrays of homogeneous data types, such as integers or floats. These arrays can be used to represent vectors, matrices, and tensors, making it easy to work with complex data structures.
2. Mathematical functions: NumPy includes a wide range of mathematical functions that can be used to perform operations on arrays. These functions include basic arithmetic operations, trigonometric functions, logarithmic functions, statistical functions, and more.
3. Broadcasting: NumPy's broadcasting feature allows for mathematical operations to be performed on arrays of different shapes and sizes, which can greatly simplify code and improve performance.
4. Integration with other libraries: NumPy is widely used in conjunction with other Python libraries for scientific computing, data analysis, and machine learning, such as SciPy, pandas, and scikit-learn.
5. Performance: NumPy is implemented in C and optimized for speed, making it much faster than traditional Python code for numerical operations. This performance advantage is particularly important when working with large datasets.

Here are some examples of how to use NumPy in Python:

1. Creating arrays: NumPy arrays can be created using the `numpy.array()` function or using one of the many other functions provided by NumPy, such as `numpy.zeros()`, `numpy.ones()`, `numpy.random.rand()`, and more.

```
import numpy as np
# Create a 1D array
arr1 = np.array([1, 2, 3, 4, 5])
print(arr1)
# Create a 2D array
arr2 = np.array([[1, 2, 3], [4, 5, 6]])
print(arr2)
```

2.Mathematical operations: NumPy provides a wide range of mathematical operations that can be performed on arrays, including addition, subtraction, multiplication, division, and more.

```python
import numpy as np
# Create two arrays
arr1 = np.array([1, 2, 3])
arr2 = np.array([4, 5, 6])
# Perform arithmetic operations
print(arr1 + arr2)
print(arr1 - arr2)
print(arr1 * arr2)
print(arr1 / arr2)
```

3. Broadcasting: NumPy's broadcasting feature allows for mathematical operations to be performed on arrays of different shapes and sizes.

```python
import numpy as np
# Create a 2D array
arr1 = np.array([[1, 2, 3], [4, 5, 6]])
# Create a 1D array
arr2 = np.array([10, 20, 30])
# Perform arithmetic operations using broadcasting
print(arr1 + arr2)
```

4. Statistical functions: NumPy provides a wide range of statistical functions that can be used to analyze and manipulate data.

```python
import numpy as np
# Create an array
arr = np.array([1, 2, 3, 4, 5])
# Compute mean, median, and standard deviation
print(np.mean(arr))
print(np.median(arr))
print(np.std(arr))
```

Some additional examples of how to use NumPy for common tasks in data analysis and machine learning:

1. Matrix operations: NumPy can be used to perform a wide range of matrix operations, such as matrix multiplication, dot products, and transpose operations.

```python
import numpy as np
# Create two matrices
matrix1 = np.array([[1, 2], [3, 4]])
matrix2 = np.array([[5, 6], [7, 8]])
# Compute matrix multiplication
print(np.matmul(matrix1, matrix2))
# Compute dot product
print(np.dot(matrix1, matrix2))
# Compute transpose
print(matrix1.T)
```

2.Indexing and slicing: NumPy provides powerful indexing and slicing operations for selecting elements or subsets of an array.

```
import numpy as np
# Create a 2D array
arr = np.array([[1, 2, 3], [4, 5, 6], [7, 8, 9]])
# Indexing
print(arr[0, 0]) # Output: 1
print(arr[2, 1]) # Output: 8
# Slicing
print(arr[1, :]) # Output: [4 5 6]
print(arr[:, 1]) # Output: [2 5 8]
```

3.Reshaping and stacking: NumPy provides functions for reshaping and stacking arrays, which can be useful for data preprocessing and manipulation.

```
import numpy as np
# Create a 1D array
arr1 = np.array([1, 2, 3, 4, 5, 6])
# Reshape into a 2D array
arr2 = arr1.reshape((2, 3))
print(arr2)
# Stack two arrays vertically
arr3 = np.array([[7, 8, 9]])
arr4 = np.vstack((arr2, arr3))
print(arr4)
# Stack two arrays horizontally
arr5 = np.array([[10], [11]])
arr6 = np.hstack((arr4, arr5))
print(arr6)
```

Conclusion

NumPy is a versatile package that can be used for a wide range of tasks in data analysis and machine learning. It provides an efficient and optimized array object, along with a wide range of mathematical functions and operations, that make it a popular choice for scientific computing in Python. By mastering NumPy, you will have a powerful tool in your data science toolbox that will enable you to efficiently manipulate and analyze large datasets.

SECTION 3

Pandas is a Python library that provides fast, flexible, and expressive data structures designed to make working with "relational" or "labeled" data both easy and intuitive. It is a popular tool for data wrangling, data analysis, and data visualization in Python.

Pandas provides two main classes for working with data: Series and DataFrame. A Series is a one-dimensional labeled array capable of holding any data type, such as integers, floats, strings, and Python objects. A DataFrame is a two-dimensional labeled data structure with columns of potentially different types, similar to a spreadsheet or SQL table. In addition, Pandas provides functions for reading and writing data to and from various file formats, including CSV, Excel, SQL databases, and more.

Here are some examples of how to use Pandas for common tasks in data analysis:

1. Reading data: Pandas provides functions for reading data from various file formats, such as CSV, Excel, and SQL databases.

```
import pandas as pd
# Read data from a CSV file
data = pd.read_csv('data.csv')
# Read data from an Excel file
data = pd.read_excel('data.xlsx')
# Read data from a SQL database
import sqlite3
conn = sqlite3.connect('example.db')
data = pd.read_sql_query('SELECT * FROM my_table', conn)
```

2. Data wrangling: Pandas provides powerful functions for cleaning, transforming, and aggregating data.

```
import pandas as pd
# Filter rows based on a condition
data = data[data['column1'] > 0]
# Rename columns
data = data.rename(columns={'old_name': 'new_name'})
# Group data by a column and compute aggregates
grouped_data = data.groupby('column1').agg(({'column2': 'mean', 'column3': 'sum'})
# Merge two dataframes based on a common column
merged_data = pd.merge(data1, data2, on='common_column')
```

3. Data visualization: Pandas provides built-in functions for creating basic visualizations of data.

```
import pandas as pd
import matplotlib.pyplot as plt
# Create a line plot of a column
data['column1'].plot()
# Create a bar chart of a column
```

```
data['column2'].plot(kind='bar')
# Create a scatter plot of two columns
data.plot(kind='scatter', x='column1', y='column2')
```

Conclusion

Pandas is a versatile library that can be used for a wide range of tasks in data analysis. It provides a powerful set of tools for reading, cleaning, transforming, and aggregating data, as well as functions for visualizing data. By mastering Pandas, you will have a powerful tool in your data science toolbox that will enable you to efficiently manipulate and analyze large datasets.

SECTION 4

Matplotlib is a popular Python library for creating high-quality data visualizations. It provides a wide range of functions for creating various types of plots, including line plots, scatter plots, bar charts, and more. In this article, we'll explore some of the key features of Matplotlib and how to use them to create effective data visualizations.

Getting Started with Matplotlib

Before we dive into creating visualizations, let's first install Matplotlib using pip:

```
pip install matplotlib
```

Now we can import Matplotlib and start creating our first plot:

```
import matplotlib.pyplot as plt
# Create some data
x = [1, 2, 3, 4, 5]
y = [2, 4, 6, 8, 10]
# Create a line plot
plt.plot(x, y)
# Show the plot
plt.show()
```

This code will create a simple line plot of our data using Matplotlib's `plot` function. We then call `show` to display the plot in a separate window.

Customizing Plots

One of the strengths of Matplotlib is its ability to customize the appearance of plots. For example, we can add a title and labels to our plot using the `title`, `xlabel`, and `ylabel` functions:

```
import matplotlib.pyplot as plt
# Create some data
x = [1, 2, 3, 4, 5]
y = [2, 4, 6, 8, 10]
# Create a line plot
plt.plot(x, y)
# Add a title and axis labels
plt.title('My Plot')
plt.xlabel('X Axis')
plt.ylabel('Y Axis')
# Show the plot
plt.show()
```

We can also customize the style of our plot using Matplotlib's built-in styles or by specifying custom settings. For example, we can use the `style` function to set the style of our plot:

```
import matplotlib.pyplot as plt
# Set the style
plt.style.use('ggplot')
# Create some data
x = [1, 2, 3, 4, 5]
y = [2, 4, 6, 8, 10]
# Create a line plot
plt.plot(x, y)
# Add a title and axis labels
plt.title('My Plot')
plt.xlabel('X Axis')
plt.ylabel('Y Axis')
# Show the plot
plt.show()
```

This code will set the style of our plot to "ggplot", which provides a clean, modern look.

Creating Different Types of Plots

Matplotlib provides a wide range of functions for creating different types of plots. Here are some examples:

```
import matplotlib.pyplot as plt
# Line plot
x = [1, 2, 3, 4, 5]
y = [2, 4, 6, 8, 10]
plt.plot(x, y)
# Scatter plot
x = [1, 2, 3, 4, 5]
y = [2, 4, 6, 8, 10]
plt.scatter(x, y)
# Bar chart
x = ['A', 'B', 'C', 'D', 'E']
y = [2, 4, 6, 8, 10]
plt.bar(x, y)
# Histogram
data = [1, 2, 3, 4, 5, 5, 5, 6, 6, 7]
plt.hist(data)
# Box plot
data = [1, 2, 3, 4, 5, 5,5, 6, 7]
plt.boxplot(data)
# Pie chart
labels = ['A', 'B', 'C', 'D', 'E'] sizes = [15, 30, 45, 10, 5] plt.pie(sizes,
labels=labels)
#Show the Plots
plt.show()
```

These are just a few examples of the many types of plots you can create with Matplotlib. Each function provides a wide range of options for customizing the appearance of your plots.

Conclusion

In this article, we've explored some of the key features of Matplotlib and how to use them to create effective data visualizations. We've seen how to create line plots, scatter plots, bar charts, histograms, box plots, and pie charts, and how to customize the appearance of our plots with titles, labels, and styles. With these tools at your disposal, you can create powerful visualizations that help you explore and communicate your data effectively.

SECTION 5

Scikit-learn is a Python library that provides a wide range of tools for machine learning. It is built on top of NumPy, SciPy, and Matplotlib, and provides a simple and efficient interface for working with machine learning algorithms.

Scikit-learn includes many popular machine learning algorithms, such as linear regression, logistic regression, support vector machines, decision trees, and random forests. It also provides tools for data preprocessing, feature selection, and model evaluation.

In this article, we will explore some of the key features of Scikit-learn and how to use them to build machine learning models.

Getting Started with Scikit-learn

Before we start building machine learning models with Scikit-learn, let's first take a look at how to install it. Scikit-learn can be installed using pip, the Python package manager, by running the following command:

```
pip install scikit-learn
```

Once Scikit-learn is installed, we can start using it in our Python programs. The first step is to import the library, which can be done using the following command:

```
import sklearn
```

Now that we have imported Scikit-learn, let's take a look at some of its key features.

Data Preprocessing with Scikit-learn

Before we can build machine learning models, we often need to preprocess our data. This involves cleaning and transforming the data to make it suitable for machine learning algorithms.

Scikit-learn provides several tools for data preprocessing, such as:

- Imputation: filling in missing values in the data
- Scaling: scaling the data so that it has zero mean and unit variance
- Encoding: converting categorical variables into numerical variables

Here is an example of how to use Scikit-learn to preprocess data:

```
from sklearn.preprocessing import Imputer, StandardScaler, LabelEncoder
# Load the data
data = [[1, 2, None], [4, None, 6], [7, 8, 9]]
```

```
# Impute missing values with the mean of the column
imputer = Imputer()
data = imputer.fit_transform(data)
# Scale the data
scaler = StandardScaler()
data = scaler.fit_transform(data)
# Encode categorical variables
encoder = LabelEncoder()
labels = ['cat', 'dog', 'dog', 'cat']
labels_encoded = encoder.fit_transform(labels)
```

In this example, we first load some data that contains missing values. We then use the Imputer class to fill in the missing values with the mean of the column. Next, we use the StandardScaler class to scale the data so that it has zero mean and unit variance. Finally, we use the LabelEncoder class to convert the categorical variable 'cat' and 'dog' into numerical variables.

Building Machine Learning Models with Scikit-learn

The iris dataset contains measurements of sepal length, sepal width, petal length, and petal width for three species of iris flowers—setosa, versicolor, and virginica. Our goal is to train a machine learning model that can predict the species of an iris flower given its measurements.

Here's how we can use Scikit-learn to achieve this goal:

Step 1: Loading the Data

We can load the iris dataset using Scikit-learn's `load_iris()` function:

```
from sklearn.datasets import load_iris
iris = load_iris()
```

The `iris` variable is a `Bunch` object that contains the dataset as well as some metadata.

Step 2: Splitting the Data into Training and Test Sets

Next, we need to split the data into training and test sets. We will use 80% of the data for training and the remaining 20% for testing. Scikit-learn provides a `train_test_split()` function that makes this easy:

```
from sklearn.model_selection import train_test_split
X_train, X_test, y_train, y_test = train_test_split(iris.data, iris.target,
test_size=0.2, random_state=42)
```

`X_train` and `y_train` are the training features and labels, respectively, while `X_test` and `y_test` are the test features and labels.

Step 3: Preprocessing the Data

Before we can train our machine learning model, we need to preprocess the data. This includes scaling the features to have zero mean and unit variance:

```
from sklearn.preprocessing import StandardScaler
scaler = StandardScaler()
X_train = scaler.fit_transform(X_train)
X_test = scaler.transform(X_test)
```

We fit the `StandardScaler` object to the training data and then use it to transform both the training and test data.

Step 4: Training the Model

We will use a Support Vector Machine (SVM) classifier to train our model. Scikit-learn provides an implementation of SVM called `svc`. We create an instance of this class and fit it to the training data:

```
from sklearn.svm import SVC
clf = SVC()
clf.fit(X_train, y_train)
```

`clf` is our trained machine learning model.

Step 5: Evaluating the Model

We can now use our trained model to make predictions on the test data:

```
y_pred = clf.predict(X_test)
```

We can evaluate the performance of our model by computing its accuracy:

```
from sklearn.metrics import accuracy_score
accuracy = accuracy_score(y_test, y_pred)
print("Accuracy:", accuracy)
```

The `accuracy_score()` function compares the predicted labels (`y_pred`) to the true labels (`y_test`) and computes the accuracy.

Conclusion

In conclusion, scikit-learn is a powerful and popular library for machine learning in Python. It provides a wide range of algorithms for classification, regression, clustering, and dimensionality reduction, as well as tools for model selection and evaluation. With its easy-to-use API and extensive documentation, scikit-learn is a great choice for beginners and experienced users alike.

Using scikit-learn, we can quickly build and evaluate machine learning models for a variety of tasks, such as predicting customer churn, detecting fraud, or classifying images. By leveraging the power of scikit-learn, we can develop robust and accurate models that can help us make better decisions and gain deeper insights into our data.

However, it is important to note that scikit-learn is just one tool in the machine learning toolkit. To be successful in machine learning, we need to have a solid understanding of the underlying concepts and principles, as well as knowledge of other libraries and tools that can help us preprocess, analyze, and visualize our data.

Overall, scikit-learn is an essential library for any data scientist or machine learning practitioner, and mastering its capabilities can help us unlock the full potential of machine learning for a wide range of applications.